Mighty Tree

Story and Pictures by **DICK GACKENBACH**

Voyager Books
Harcourt Brace & Company

San Diego   New York   London

Requests for permission to make copies of any part of
the work should be mailed to: Permissions Department,
Harcourt Brace & Company, 6277 Sea Harbor Drive,
Orlando, Florida 32887-6777.

First Voyager Books edition 1996

Voyager Books is a registered trademark of Harcourt Brace & Company.

The Library of Congress has cataloged the hardcover edition as follows:
Gackenbach, Dick.
Mighty tree/story and pictures by Dick Gackenbach.—1st ed.
p.   cm.
Summary: Three seeds grow into three beautiful trees,
each of which serves a different function in nature and for
people.
ISBN 0-15-200519-6
ISBN 0-15-201013-0 pb
1. Trees—Juvenile literature.   [1. Trees.]   I. Title.
QK475.8.G33   1992
582.16—dc20   91-12904

G F E D C B

Printed in Singapore

for Hugh Holt

Some time ago,
the wind blew three tiny seeds
to earth.

From these seeds
three small trees
began to grow.

The sun gave them warmth.
The rain gave them water,
and the earth gave them food.
Storm winds gave them shape
and made them strong.

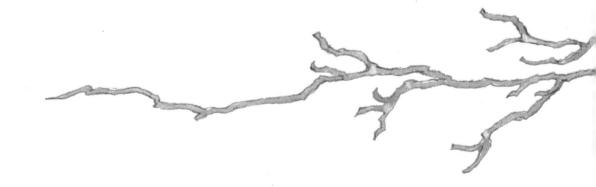

The trees grew
and grew and grew
until their crowns
nearly touched the clouds.

One summer day a big red truck
came to the quiet forest
and took one tree away.
The truck carried the tree
to a mill where it was changed
into many things.

The tree became paper to draw on
and paper to wrap presents in.

It became candy wrappers
and paper hats.

The tree became cardboard boxes
and shopping bags
and even this book.

In the winter
a big blue truck came
and took the second tree away.
The blue truck carried
the beautiful tree
to a big city.

There the tree
was covered
with stars and horns
and angels and shiny balls.
It was covered with
lights that sparkled
and glittered
and brightened
the snowy nights.

The beautiful tree
filled the hearts
of millions of people
with kindness and cheer,

and it brought smiles
to the faces
of children.

The third tree
still stands in the woods today,
and it is the most important
tree of all.

This tree is
home and shelter
to hornets,
honeybees, ladybugs,
spiders, crickets, ants,
katydids and caterpillars,
pheasants and quail
and mourning doves,

woodpeckers and flickers,
squirrels and chipmunks,
and even sleeping bears.

It is home to lizards,
opossums and raccoons,
runaway kites
and butterfly cocoons
and bluejays and robins,
cardinals and crows.
Chickadees,
crossbills and titmice,
nuthatches and bluebirds
and owls and hawks
and eagles, too,
all find shelter in its branches.

The mighty tree stands there still,
sending out its tiny seeds
to blow in the wind.

The illustrations in this book were done in pen and ink and Dr. Martin's
Radiant Concentrated Watercolors on D'Arches 140-lb. cold press watercolor paper.

The text type was set in ITC New Baskerville by Typelink, San Diego, California.

The display type was set in Americana Bold by Thompson Type, San Diego,
California.

Printed and bound by Tien Wah Press, Singapore

This book was printed on Arctic matte paper.

Designed by Trina Stahl

Production supervision by Warren Wallerstein and Diana Ford